Simple Dumpling and Gyoza Recipe Book

Delicious Dumpling Gyoza Recipes for Beginners and Beyond

G000039056

Table of Contents

Introduction

Everywhere In the world you visit, dumplings vary. They vary in cooking technique, ingredients and taste, in this Gyoza Cookbook, we will be exploring and preparing a variety of recipes from all over the world. Certainly, we will be taking a world tour which will feature dumpling recipes from the Caribbean – West Indian dumplings; Asia – Asian dumplings; America – North American dumplings and Africa – South African dumplings.

If you don't embark on this tour with us, you will really be missing out on some great recipes so, get your copy of this great cookbook and have some fun in your kitchen!

Traditional Gyoza

This is a pork based dim sum recipe having garlic and chili flavors.

Serves: 10

Time: 25 minutes

Ingredients:

- Ground pork: 1 lb.
- Green cabbage chopped: 1 lb.
- Ginger garlic: 2 tbsp each

- Soy sauce: ¼ cup
- Sugar: 1 tbsp
- Wonton wrappers: 2 packages
- Vegetable oil: 1 tsp
- Gyoza: 12
- Hot water
- Basic dipping sauce
- **For dipping sauce:**
- Soy sauce: 2 tbsp
- Rice wine vinegar: 1 tbsp
- Sesame oil: ¼ tsp

Directions

1. Take a bowl and mix pork, garlic, cabbage, soy sauce, ginger and sugar. Fry the patty made from this into the pan with seasoning.

2. Brush wonton skin with water and put into meat mixture in center, fold and seal the skin into half-moon shape.

3. Make rest of dumplings, then cover and refrigerate for an hour.

4. Take a skillet and brown gyoza in heated oil for a few minutes.

5. Add hot water to cover dumplings and cook for 7 minutes.

6. Serve with the dipping sauce made by combining dipping sauce ingredients.

Vegetable Style Pan Fried Dumplings

If you are looking for a healthy dumpling recipe to make, this is the perfect dish for you. I know you are going to love it.

Serves: 24

Time: 1 hr.

Ingredients:

Your Filling:

- ½ Cup of Carrot, Fresh and Finely Diced
- ½ Cup of Tofu, Five Spice Variety and Finely Diced

- ½ Cup of Seitan, Finely Diced
- ¼ Ounce of Mushrooms, Wood Ear Variety, Dried, Rehydrated and Finely Diced
- 1 Cup of Cabbage, Roughly Diced
- 2 tbsp of Garlic, Minced
- 1 tbsp of Scallions, White Parts Only and Minced
- ½ tsp of Sugar, White
- 2 tsp of Oil, Sesame Variety
- 2 tsp of Soy Sauce, Your Favorite Kind

Your Dumplings:

- ½ tsp of White Pepper, For Taste
- ¼ tsp of Salt, For Taste
- 2 tsp of Cornstarch
- 24 Dumpling Skins, Prepackaged
- 1 tbsp of Oil, Vegetable Variety
- Your Dipping Sauce:
- 1 teaspoon of Oil, Sesame Variety
- 4 tsp of Soy Sauce, Light and Your Favorite Kind
- 2 tsp of Vinegar, Rice Variety
- 1 Scallion, Finely Sliced

Directions:

1. Mix all of your ingredients for your filling together in a large sized bowl until thoroughly mixed together.

2. Next roll out your dumpling wrappers and drizzle the edges with some water.

3. Place your filling by the spoonful into the center of your wrappers and cover. Seal the edges with a fork. Repeat with remaining wrappers and filling.

4. Next heat up some oil in a large skillet placed over high heat. Once your oil is simmering add in your dumplings and cook for the next couple of minutes or until brown and golden in color.

5. Then slightly reduce the heat to low and continue cooking the dumplings for the next 6 to 8 minutes before removing from heat.

6. Then mix together all of your ingredients for your dipping sauce in a small sized bowl until evenly mixed together and smooth inconsistency. Serve with your dumplings and enjoy.

Jiu Cai He Zi Dumplings

In China, a Jiu Cai He Zi is a pan-fried Chinese pancake filled with chives and scrambled eggs.

Serves: 4

Time: 1 hr. 30 mins.

Ingredients:

- Flour (2 cups)
- Water (1 cup, lukewarm)
- Baking Powder (3 tsp.)
- Salt (1/2 tsp for dough, 1 tsp for eggs)

- Garlic Chives (4oz, finely chopped)
- Eggs (3, beaten)
- Vermicelli (1oz., soaked and softened)
- Sesame Oil (1 tsp)
- Ground Pork (1/2 lbs., cooked)
- White Pepper (1/4 tsp)

Directions:

1. To create your dough, add all your dry ingredients to a large bowl, and stir with your hand until fully combined.

2. Next gradually add water, kneading until it forms the dough.

NB: Your dough will be ready when it bounces back after a gentle touch. If the dough appears to be too dry, then add a bit more water but be careful not to make it too sticky.

3. Cover all the dough with a plastic wrap and let stand for about 30 minutes.

4. In a non-stick pan over medium high heat, lightly brush it with oil and set your eggs to scramble or create a very thinly layer of lightly fried egg with little to no color, then chop it up into thin pieces and set aside.

5. Next chop up your softened vermicelli noodles and chives so that they are small pieces (similar to the size of your scrambled or chopped eggs).

6. In a medium bowl, combine your pork, vermicelli, eggs, chives, salt as well as pepper and mix until fully combined. Ensure that it is seasoned enough for your liking.

7. Now to assemble our dumplings: Divide your dough into 12 equal pieces and roll each piece out into a thin square.

8. Next add 2 tbsp of your filling mixture into the middle of each square. Fold the far end of the bottom right of the square to meet the diagonal opposite to the top left of the dough square, then repeat the same process on the opposite side. Next pinch the dumpling to seal all the openings, creating a fully pleated dumpling.

9. Coat both sides of the dumpling with oil lightly. Lay them on a non-stick skillet and pour about 1/4 cup of water in the pan, set over high heat and bring to a boil.

10. Once boiling, reduce the temperature to the medium-low and continue to cook until all the water evaporated.

11. Once all the water has evaporated, reduce the heat to the lowest setting and continue to cook dumplings, turning periodically until they are evenly brown on all sides. Serve and Enjoy!

Vegetarian Dumplings

If you want some classic vegetarian dumpling recipe, try this amazing combo of mushrooms and other vegetables.

Serve: 6

Time: 1 hour 15 minutes

Ingredients:

- Olive oil: 3 tbsp
- Chopped mushrooms: 1 lb.
- Chopped garlic: 4 cloves
- Grated carrot: ½ cup
- Soy sauce: 1 tbsp

- Sesame oil: 2 tbsp
- Sriracha: 1 tsp
- Black pepper: ½ tsp
- Green onion, sliced: 1

Directions:

1. Take a skillet and heat oil. Cook garlic and mushrooms for 10 minutes. Stir in cabbage and carrots and cook for 2 minutes.

2. Remove from heat, and then add sesame oil, soy sauce, green onion and pepper.

3. Put filling into wrappers and shape, then seal in a half moon shape. Cover dumplings with tower and refrigerate for an hour.

4. Take a skillet and heat 1 tbsp vegetable oil on medium heat.

5. Fry dumplings for 4 minutes. Then add water and reduce heat.

6. Cover and cook for 3 minutes.

7. Serve with soy sauce.

Rose Dumplings

It's a traditional recipe in Chinese cuisine and served in breakfast and lunch mostly. It's refreshing and yummy.

Serve: 8

Time: 25 minutes

Ingredients:

- Flour: 2 cups
- Egg: 1
- Roses: 8
- Carrot: ½

- Mushrooms: 2
- Diced wood ear: 1 piece
- Oyster sauce: 1 tbsp
- Dry tofu: 1 cup
- Soy sauce: 1 tbsp
- Olive oil: 1 tsp
- Ginger root: 1

Directions:

1. Take a pot, mix lukewarm water with wood wear, tofu and mushrooms. Let them soak.

2. Take another bowl, mix flour and corn flour with water.

3. Knead dough for 20 minutes, chop carrots and soaked ingredients.

4. Beat eggs in a bowl and mix all these fillings in a single bowl.

5. Make dumplings out of dough and shape these into a triangle.

6. Leave a little hole in mid to decorate with rose.

7. Steam dumplings in boiling water steamer for 20 minutes. Enjoy!

Chinese rice dumplings – 'Zongzi'

This recipe has been made with glutinous rice stuffed with different fillings.

Serve: 6

Time needed: 1 hr. 10 minutes

Ingredients:

- Glutinous Rice: ½ lb.
- Chinese dates: 1-2 oz.
- Bamboo leaves
- Cotton thread

Directions:

Wash bamboo leaves and soak both leaves and rice overnight. Drain before using. Fold two leaves in a funnel shape and put rice in the bottom. Then add in Chinese dates and again cover with rice. Fold down leaves and seal with thread. Take a pot and boil water with Zongzi (rice dumplings) for an hour on medium heat. Serve.

Chive and Prawn Potstickers

This is a refreshing fried dumpling to enjoy, giving an amazing combination of prawns and chive.

Serve: 4

Time: 40 minutes

Ingredients:

- Shrimps, peeled and minced: 2 cups

- Chinese chives: chopped: 3 tbsp
- Oyster sauce: 1 tbsp
- Shaohsing rice wine: 1 tbsp
- Sea salt white pepper
- Dumpling wrappers: 30
- Peanut oil: 2 tbsp
- Corn flour

Directions:

1. Take a bowl and mix all filling ingredients.

2. Put some corn flour in a tray. Have a dumpling wrapper in your palm and put some filling; press and seal wrapper in a half moon shape.

3. Put all potstickers this way. Take a skillet and heat oil.

4. Cook for 5 to 7 minutes. Then add water till edges of the skillet.

5. Cover and cook for another 10 minutes.

6. Serve and enjoy.

Prawn Pork Dumplings

Get this unique combo of pork and prawns, filled with interesting and new flavors.

Serve: 8

Time: 35 minutes

Ingredients:

- Ground pork: 15 g
- Raw prawns, coarsely diced: 115 g
- Spring Onion chopped: 1

- Grated Ginger: 1 tbsp
- Soy sauce: 1 tbsp.+ 2 tbsp
- Rice wine: 1 tbsp
- Corn flour: 2 tbsp
- Sesame oil: 1 tsp
- Sea salt black pepper
- Dumpling wrappers: 10
- Chili sauce: 1 tbsp

Directions:

1. Take a bowl and mix onion, ginger, prawns, pork, soy sauce, rice wine, salt, pepper, corn flour, and sesame oil.

2. Take a dumpling wrapper and put in fillings.

3. Shape and seal the wrapper into half-moon shape.

4. Heat oil in a bamboo steamer bottom and place parchment paper.

5. Arrange dumplings in steamer, then cover and cook for 8 minutes.

6. Serve with chili sauce and soy sauce dip.

Beef Dumplings

Ground Beef go great in these dumplings too.

Serve: 8

Time: 35 mins.

Ingredients:

- Ground beef: 15 g
- Spring Onion chopped: 1
- Ginger powder: 1 tbsp
- Soy sauce: 1 tbsp + 2 tbsp
- Rice wine: 1 tbsp
- Corn flour: 2 tbsp

- Sesame oil: 1 tsp
- Sea salt black pepper
- Dumpling wrappers: 10
- Chili sauce: 1 tbsp

Directions:

1. Take a bowl and mix onion, ginger powder, beef, soy sauce, rice wine, salt and pepper, corn flour and sesame oil.

2. Take a dumpling wrapper and put in fillings. Shape and seal the wrapper into half moon shape.

3. Heat oil in a bamboo steamer bottom and place parchment paper. Arrange dumplings in steamer, then cover and cook for 8 minutes.

4. Serve with chili sauce and soy sauce dip.

Jian Jiao

Jian Jiao is a pan-fried dumpling, usually made from eggs cooked into an omelette with meat filling inside, which is usually served during Chinese New Year.

Serves: 6-8

Time: 1 hr.

Ingredients:

Filling:

- ½ cup of ground chicken
- 1 tbsp of Shaoxing wine

- 1 pinch of salt
- 2 stalks of finely diced spring onion
- 1 pinch of white pepper
- 1/2 tbsp of sesame oil.
- Dumpling Wrapper:
- 4 eggs
- 1 tbsp of corn starch
- 1/2 tbsp of water.

Sauce:

- 2 tbsp of soy sauce
- 1tbsp of Shaoxing wine
- 2 cups of water
- 1 pinch of salt and sugar
- 1 tbsp of water
- 1 tbsp of corn starch.

Directions:

1. For filling, mix all the ingredients together and set aside for 30minutes.

2. Beat the eggs and mix the water and cornstarch. Preheat a non-stick pan with some oil.

3. Add 1 tbsp of the egg mixture and disperse it on the pan with a spoon to form a circular shape of about 3-inch. Ensure the egg mixture is "thick" enough to do this.

4. When the bottom is cooked, and the top is still wet, add about one tsp of the filling in the middle of the egg, and then bend/fold the egg over it; tightly press the edges gently, so it seals.

5. A half circle is formed at this stage. Uncooked the filling at this point and repeat until you are done with the eggs and filling.

6. Put the sauce ingredients (except for cornstarch mixture) in a medium size pot with a lid and bring it to boil.

7. You can have a taste and adjust to your liking and then add the egg dumplings made above.

8. Reduce the heat and cover, then cook it gently for 15 minutes. Next, add your cornstarch mixture, then bring it back to boil, stirring till it gets thickened. Turn off the heat and serve immediately.

Sui Kow

This recipe marries shrimp, oyster sauce and pork together in one delicious dumpling.

Serves: 12

Time: 1 hr.

Ingredients:

- 160g medium size shrimps
- 80g semi-lean pork (minced)
- 1 tbsp of coriander leaves (use the leaves only and must be finely diced)
- 25 pieces of round-shaped dumpling wrappers
- 3 parts of water chestnuts

- 30g carrots
- 2 pieces of dried mushrooms
- water for boiling
- 1 handful of diced spring onions
- 1 handful of frozen green peas

Seasonings:

- 2 tbsp of oyster sauce
- 2 tsp of corn starch
- 1 teaspoon of sesame oil
- 1 teaspoon of cooking oil
- 1teaspoon of salt,
- 1teaspoon of sugar
- 1 dash white pepper

Directions:

Filling:

1. Rinse the prawns, devein and peel under a running tap, then dry with a kitchen towel.

2. Split them into 2 equal portions. In the 1st portion – put 1 shrimp on a chopping board and smash hit to flatten it.

3. Repeat the same method for all the shrimps. Chop your shrimps with the back of a chopper till it is fine and sticky.

4. Beat lightly till a paste is formed. In the 2nd portion – it is chopped roughly into smaller chunks.

5. Now, wash and soak the mushrooms in water to get softer, then drain and squeeze dry.

6. Next chop your water chestnuts, carrots, and soaked mushrooms into fine cubes.

7. Combine the seasoning and all the ingredients in a large mixing bowl and stir until combined, going only in one direction.

8. Use plastic wrap to cover the bowl then set aside in the refrigerator to cool for about two hours.

Wrapping Cooking:

1. Prepare a clean cloth to wipe, clean and dry your hands. Gradually place the dumpling wrapper on your palm and put one tsp of filling in the center of the wrapper.

2. Wet the wrapper's edge, fold it in half then press firmly. Lightly dust a tray with flour then top your tray with your filled wrappers. Set a large pot with water on to boil.

3. The dumplings are divided into two batches and placed beside each other. Stir in a clockwise direction to prevent the dumplings from sticking together.

4. Boil again and reduce the heat to low to keep cooking (without cover) with medium heat and allow it to boil again.

5. Repeat the process until the filling is cooked, so as to prevent the wrapper from breaking and make the cooked filling tenderer.

6. Turn off the heat when the dumpling is cooked and place them in a serving bowl with sesame oil sprinkled on it.

7. Pour some broth over the dumplings and garnish with the diced spring onion and dash of white pepper powder. Then, serve immediately.

Shui Jiao

Light and delicious dumplings generally served in soups.

Serves: 10

Time: 1 hr. 30 mins.

Ingredients:

- Sesame Oil (4 tbsp 1 tsp.)
- Soy Sauce (4 tbsp.)

- Black Vinegar (2 tbsp.)
- Garlic (3½ oz.)
- Scallions (1½ cups, finely chopped)
- Mushroom powder (2 tsp.)
- Corn Starch (1 tsp.)
- Salt (1 tsp.)
- Ginger (1/2 tsp., grated)
- Black Pepper (½ tsp.)
- Wonton wrappers (30, 4 ½ inch, round)
- Pork (1 lb., ground)

Directions:

1. In your small bowl, mix together 1 teaspoon of soy sauce, vinegar and sesame oil, then set aside.

2. Next prepare a baking sheet by adding a parchment paper to it and sprinkling it with flour.

3. Also set aside a baking sheet with parchment paper and sprinkle it with flour. Combine all your remaining ingredients in a large bowl and stir forcefully to combine.

4. Next, assemble your dumplings by adding a tbsp of pork filling onto the middle of the wrapper, rubbing water on the

other edges of the wrapper, then folding it in half with a damp cloth, while you work on the remaining dumplings.

5. Set a pot of water on to boil and add salt to taste. Once boiling, add your dumpling in and allow to cook on medium heat until fully cooked (about 8 minutes). Serve with sesame oil sauce that you set aside earlier and enjoy.

Gyoza Sauce

The perfect dipping sauce. So much better than store-bought.

Serves: ¾ cup

Time: 45 mins.

Ingredients:

- 1/3 cup rice vinegar
- 1/3 cup soy sauce
- 1 tbsp chili garlic sauce
- 2 minced garlic cloves
- 2 tbsp sugar

- 1 tsp grated ginger
- 3 tsp chopped scallion
- 1 tbsp sesame seed oil

Directions:

1. Combine all ingredients well.

2. Chill for 30 minutes.

Potstickers

The secret to these perfect potstickers is to grate the vegetables very fine and not to cook them beforehand. Serve with one of the dipping sauces in this book.

Serves: 4

Time: 19 mins.

Ingredients:

- 2 tbsp sesame oil
- 2 cups finely chopped cabbage
- 1/4 cup minced scallions
- 2 minced garlic cloves
- 2 tbsp grated ginger
- ¼ cup grated carrots
- ½ lb. ground pork
- 1 tbsp sake
- wonton wrappers, 1 package
- ¼ cup water

Directions:

1. Heat the sesame oil in a skillet. Stir in the ground pork and sake and cook for 8 minutes, until the pork is no longer pink.

2. Place the pork in a bowl and stir in all the vegetables. Fill each wonton wrapper with a tbsp of filling.

3. Moisten fingertips in the water and close the wrapper by folding it.

Continue until all wrappers are used.

4. Cook the gyozas for 1 minute on each side in the hot oil.

8. Pour ¼ cup water in the skillet and simmer the gyoza for 10 minutes.

Delicious Shrimp Packed Dumplings

If you are a huge fan of shrimp and are looking for a healthy and delicious recipe to make, this is the perfect dish to make. These dumplings are plump and juicy, making them extremely satisfying.

Serves: 25

Time: 1 hr.

Ingredients:

Your Dough:

- ½ Cup of Water, Warm
- ¾ Cup of Starch, Wheat Variety
- 6 tbsp of Flour, Tapioca Variety
- 1/8 tsp of Salt, For Taste
- 2 tsp of Oil, Canola Variety

Your Shrimp Filling:

- ½ Pound of Shrimp, Shelled and Deveined
- 1 teaspoon of Baker's Style Baking Sofa
- 1, 2 Inch Piece of Pork Fatback
- ½ tsp of Ginger, Minced
- ½ tsp of Garlic, Minced
- ½ tsp of Wine, Shaoxing Variety
- ¼ tsp of Salt, For Taste
- ¼ tsp of Sugar, White
- ¼ tsp of Pepper, White in Color and Ground
- 1 teaspoon of Oil, Vegetable Variety
- 1 teaspoon of Cornstarch
- Some Vinegar, Black in Color and for Serving
- **Directions**:

1. The first thing that you want to do is mix all of your ingredients for your filling together in a large sized bowl until thoroughly mixed together.

2. Then mix together all of your ingredients for your dough in a large sized bowl until your mixture forms a sticky dough. Cover with some plastic wrap and set aside for later use.

3. Roll out your dough and cut into small sized wrappers. Fill your wrappers with your filling and fold to seal the edges. Crimp the edges with your fork and sprinkle with some water.

4. Next heat up some oil in a large skillet placed over high heat. Once your oil is hot enough add in your dumplings and cook for the next couple of minutes or until brown in color.

5. Then slightly reduce the heat to low and continue cooking the dumplings for the next 6 to 8 minutes before removing from heat and enjoying whenever you are ready.

Black Sesame Dumplings

You can opt to have these dumplings in plain water but to truly get the sweet dessert feeling from them, you need to have them with natural ginger made syrup.

Serves: 4

Time: 40 minutes

Ingredients:

- Glutinous rice flour (8oz)
- Water (3/4 cup)

- Black sesame seeds (1/4 cup)
- Sugar (1/4 cup)
- Butter-unsalted (1/4 cup)
- -Ginger Syrup (1/4 tsp)
- Water (5 cups)
- Sugar (1 cup)
- Ginger (4 oz.)
- Screwpine leaves (2, optional)

Directions:

1. Toast seeds over a medium fire until the sesame seeds become scented. Make sure you cover the pan used as seeds may burst.

2. Remove from flame when seeds get aromatic. Use a processor to combine seeds till they become fine.

3. Put seeds into the pan and add butter as well as sugar, combine to make a paste.

4. Add more butter if needed; put into a container and refrigerate. Mix flour with water and mix into a smooth paste. The paste should not stick to your hands.

5. Divide into 16 balls. Make each ball flat and take a few seeds, using chopsticks to place into a paste.

6. Pick up edges and pull together, then roll balls as smoothly as you can. Repeat till all paste is used up.

7. Make ginger syrup by adding ginger and sugar to 5 cups of boiling water. Boil until water has been condensed by 1 cup, you may add more sugar if so desired.

8. Using another pot, put some water to boil and plunge dumplings into the water.

9. As soon as they drift to the top of the water, remove from the pot into syrup.

10. Remove syrup from the flame and serve.

Classic Chicken and Dumplings

This is yet another dumpling recipe that I know you are just going to love making. It is incredibly filling and makes for a great tasting dinner that the entire family will fall in love with.

Serves: 4 to 6

Time: 1 hr. 20 mins.

Ingredients:

Your Chicken:

- 1, 2 ½ Pound Chicken, Cut into Small Sized Pieces
- 3 Ribs of Celery, Finely Chopped and Fresh
- 1 Onion, Large in Size and Finely Chopped
- 2 Bay Leaves, Fresh and Dried
- 2 Bouillon Cubes, Chicken Variety
- 1, 10 ¾ Ounce Can of Cream of Chicken Soup, Condensed
- 1 teaspoon of House Seasoning

Your Dumplings:

- 2 Cups of Flour, All Purpose Variety
- 1 teaspoon of Salt, For Taste
- Some Water, Ice and as Needed

Your House Seasoning:

- ¼ Cup of Garlic, Powdered Variety
- ¼ Cup of Black Pepper, For Taste
- 1 Cup of Salt, For Taste

Directions:

1. First, you have to cook your chicken. To do this place your chicken along with your next 4 ingredients into a large sized pot.

2. Add in four quarts of water and allow your mixture to come to a simmer.

3. Allow your chicken to simmer for the next 40 minutes or until your chicken is completely cooked through.

4. After this time remove the skin from your chicken and return it back to the pot. Keep warm over low heat.

5. Then prepare your dumplings. To do this mix together your ingredients for your dumplings in a large sized mixing bowl.

6. Then use your fingers to knead the dough into a small sized ball and break it off into even sized dumplings.

7. Next add in your soup to your pot with your chicken and allow to continue simmering over low heat.

8. Drop your dumplings into your soup and allow to cook until your dumplings begin to float to the top. That should take about 5 minutes.

9. Remove from heat and served whenever you are ready.

Easy Rolled Dumplings

Seeking a great tasting addition to add to any broth or soup dish that you make, then this is for you. Easy to make and absolutely delicious, I know you will want to make it over and over again.

Serves: 7

Time: 25 mins.

Ingredients:

- 2 tsp of Baker's Style Baking Powder
- 2 Cups of Flour, All Purpose Variety

- 1 teaspoon of Salt, For Taste
- 1/3 Cup of Shortening, Vegetable Variety
- ½ Cup of Milk, Whole
- 2, 14.5 Ounce Cans of Chicken Broth, Homemade Preferable

Directions:

1. First combine your first three ingredients together in a large sized bowl. Cut in your shortening and add in enough milk to make a soft dough.

2. Roll out your dough until slightly thick and then cut into small squares.

3. Sprinkle your dough with some flour and drop by the tbsp into some chicken stock.

4. Cover and allow to boil for the next eight to ten minutes before removing from heat and serving.

Classic Herbed Dumplings

Here is classic herbed dumpling recipe that I know you are going to love. This is a dumpling recipe that you can make for any soup dish that you make or stew that you want to add a little extra flavor to.

Serves: 6

Time: 20 mins.

Ingredients:

- 1 ½ Cups of Flour, All Purpose Variety
- 1 teaspoon of Salt, For Taste

- 1 teaspoon of Baker's Style Baking Soda
- 2 tsp of Baker's Style Baking Powder
- 1 teaspoon of Thyme, Dried
- 1 teaspoon of Parsley, Dried
- 1 teaspoon of Oregano, Dried
- 3 tbsp of Butter, Soft
- ¾ Cup of Milk, Whole

Directions:

1. Combine your first 7 ingredients together until thoroughly combined.

2. Then cut your butter into your mixture until you have a few coarse crumbs in your bowl.

3. Gradually add in your milk then stir until a thick batter forms in your in your hands.

4. Then drop your batter by the tbsp into a simmering soup or stew and allow to cook while covered for the next 15 minutes.

5. Serve whenever you are ready and enjoy.

Hearty Pork and Cabbage Dumplings

Here is yet another Chinese classic dumpling dish that I know you are going to love. It is filled with moist and juicy pork and healthy cabbage that you won't be able to resist.

Serves: 40 to 50

Time: 1 hr.

Ingredients:

Your Dumplings:

- 1 Pound of Cabbage, Napa Variety and Finely Minced

- 1 tbsp of Salt, For Taste and Evenly Divided

- 1 Pound of Pork Shoulder, Ground

- 1 teaspoon of Pepper, White in Color and for Taste

- 1 tbsp of Garlic, Fresh and Minced

- 1 teaspoon of Ginger, Fresh and Minced

- 2 Ounces of Scallions, Minced

- 2 tsp of Sugar, White

- 1 Pack of Dumpling Wrappers, 40 to 50 at least

- Some Oil, Canola Variety and for Cooking

Your Sauce:

- ½ Cup of Vinegar, Rice Variety

- ¼ Cup of Soy Sauce, Your Favorite Kind

- 2 tbsp of Oil, Chili Variety and Optional

Directions:

1. Firstly, you have to mix all of your ingredients for your filling together in a large sized bowl until thoroughly mixed together.

2. Next roll out your dumpling wrappers and drizzle the edges with some water.

3. Place your filling by the spoonful into the center of your wrappers and cover. Seal the edges with a fork. Repeat with remaining wrappers and filling.

4. Next heat up some oil in a large sized skillet placed over high heat. Once your oil is hot enough add in your dumplings and cook for the next couple of minutes or until brown in color.

5. Then reduce the heat to low and continue cooking the dumplings for the next 6 to 8 minutes before removing from heat and enjoying whenever you are ready.

6. Then mix together all of your ingredients for your dipping sauce in a small sized bowl until evenly mixed together and smooth in consistency. Serve with your dumplings and enjoy.

Mushroom "Siu Mai" and steamed pork Dumplings

This is one of the classical dim sum creations, with sharp flavors of spices and mixture of prawn with mushrooms.

Serve: 10

Time: 35 minutes

Ingredients:

- Ground pork: 115 g
- Shiitake mushrooms chopped: 3
- Spring onion, chopped: 1

- Grated Ginger: 1 tbsp
- Soy sauce: 1 tbsp
- Shaohsing rice wine: 1 tbsp
- Sesame oil: 1 tbsp
- Sea salt pepper
- Corn flour: 2 tsp
- Dumpling wrappers: 10
- Goji berries: 15
- Vegetable oil: 1 tbsp

Directions:

Take a bowl and mix all filling ingredients. Put some filling in mid of dumpling wrapper, shape and seal wrapper into a ball shape. Heat oil in a bamboo steamer bottom and place parchment paper. Arrange dumplings in steamer, then cover and cook for 8 minutes.

Delicious Mascarpone and Butternut Gnocchi

If you don't like traditional potato style gnocchi dumplings, then this is a dish that you need to try to make for yourself. This dish features healthy butternut squash and mascarpone cheese, making it a perfect dish to leave you feeling full and satisfied.

Serves: 12

Time: 9 hrs.

Ingredients:

- 1 Pound of Butternut Squash, Fresh
- 1 Cup of Mascarpone Cheese
- ½ Cup of Parmigiano-Reggiano Cheese, Finely Grated
- 2 Eggs, Large in Size and Beaten Lightly
- 1 ½ tsp of Salt, For Taste
- ½ tsp of Black Pepper, For Taste
- 1 Cup of Flour, All Purpose Variety and Evenly Divided
- ½ Cup of Butter, Unsalted Variety and Soft
- Dash of Cayenne Pepper
- Dash of Salt, For Taste
- Dash of Pepper, For Taste
- ¼ Cup of Sage Leaves, Fresh and Thinly Sliced
- 1 tbsp of Parmigiano-Reggiano Cheese, Finely Grated

Directions:

1. The first thing you want to do this place your butternut squash into a microwave safe dish and cover with some plastic wrap.

2. Microwave for the next 8 minutes or until tender to the touch. Remove and set aside for later use.

3. Next whisk together your next five ingredients in a large sized bowl until smooth in consistency. Then add in your butternut squash and whisk again until thoroughly blended.

4. Then add in half of your flour and whisk until evenly incorporated. Add in your remaining flour and continue to stir until thoroughly combined. Cover with some plastic wrap and place into your fridge to chill for at least 8 hours.

5. The next day bring a large sized pot of water to a boil. Then use a large sized skillet and melt your butter in it over medium heat.

6. Next scoop out a tbsp of your butternut mixture and drop it gently into your boiling water. Repeat with remaining mixture until all of your mixture has been used up. Once your dumplings rise to the surface continue to cook for at least one minute in your water and then remove to drain in a plate lined with paper towels.

7. Once drained put your dumplings into your skillet with the melted butter and cook until golden brown in color on each side.

8. Season with your seasonings and garnish with your sage placed on the top. Serve whenever you are ready.

Czech Style Dumplings with Sauerkraut

This Czech style dumpling recipe is one of the most traditional ways that you can enjoy dumplings today. Either way I know you are going to love it.

Serves: 8

Time: 1 hr. 30 mins.

Ingredients:

- 3 Cups of Flour, All Purpose Variety

- 1 teaspoon of Baker's Style Baking Soda
- 1 teaspoon of Baker's Style Baking Powder
- ½ tsp of Salt, For Taste
- ½ tsp of Sugar, White
- 3 Eggs, Large in Size and Beaten Lightly
- 1 ½ Cups of Milk, Whole
- 4 Cups of Bread, White, Dry and Cut into Small Cubes
- 4 Slices of Bacon, Sliced into Small Strips
- 1, 16 Ounce Jar of Sauerkraut, Rinsed and Drained
- Dash of Salt, For Taste
- Dash of Pepper, For Taste
- 1 teaspoon of Caraway Seeds
- 2 tsp of Water, Cold
- 1 teaspoon of Cornstarch

Directions:

1. Use a large sized bowl and mix together your first five ingredients until thoroughly combined.

2. Then make a well into the center of your dough and add in your eggs with your milk. Stir thoroughly to combine and continue to add more milk to make a moist dough.

3. Next add in your white bread and stir enough until your break begins to disappear in the dough.

4. Then bring a large size pot of water to a boil over high heat. While your water is boiling press your dough into a cheesecloth and form it into a loaf shape. Make sure to wrap the cloth around your loaf and tie the ends to seal.

5. Add your loaf to your boiling water and cook for the next 45 minutes making sure to turn your loaf at least halfway through the cooking process. After this time remove from the water and allow to stand to dry for at least 10 minutes.

6. While your loaf is resting fry up your bacon in a small-sized skillet placed over medium to high heat until brown and crispy. Remove from pan and set aside.

7. Add in your sauerkraut and add enough water just to cover the surface. Allow to simmer over medium heat.

8. Add your bacon back into your pan with your remaining ingredients and simmer for the next couple of minutes until thick in consistency.

9. Slice your dumpling loaf and drizzle with your roast drippings and sauerkraut. Enjoy!

German Style Dumplings

This homemade dumpling recipe is a great dish to make to accompany any soup or chicken recipe that you may make.

Serves: 12

Time: 1 hr. 35 mins.

Ingredients:

- ¾ Cup of Milk, Whole
- ½ tsp of Salt, For Taste
- 1 ½ tbsp of Flour, All Purpose Variety

- ½ Cup of Water, Cold
- 1 Cup of Flour, All Purpose Variety
- 3 Eggs, Large in Size and Lightly Beaten
- 1 Cup of Flour, All Purpose Variety

Directions:

1. Place your milk and salt into a saucepan and heat over medium heat.

2. Then use a small-sized bowl and mix together your flour and water until thoroughly combined.

3. Add into your saucepan once and once your milk begins to bubble add in your flour mixture and continue to cook until thick inconsistency. This should take at least 2 to 3 minutes. Remove from heat and allow to cool.

4. Once your mixture is cooled fold your eggs into your dough and add in another cup of flour.

5. Drop your dough by the teaspoon into your saucepan and allow to simmer for at least 10 minutes more. Remove from heat and serve whenever you are ready.

Classic Pork Dumplings

With the help of this recipe you will never have to order traditional pork dumplings from your favorite Chinese restaurant again.

Serves: 70 to 80

Time: 30 mins.

Ingredients:

- ½ a Head of Cabbage, Napa Variety and Roughly Chopped
- 1 tbsp of Salt, For Taste
- 1 Pound of Pork, Ground and Lean
- 1 Cup of Scallions, Sliced Thinly
- ¾ Cup of Cilantro, Fresh and Minced
- 3 tbsp of Soy Sauce, Your Favorite Kind
- 1, 2 Inch Piece of Ginger, Fresh and Finely Grated
- 2 tbsp of Oil, Sesame Variety
- 2 Eggs, Large in Size and Whisked Thoroughly
- 1, 12 Ounce Pack of Dumpling Wrappers, Round in Size

Directions:

1. Slice your cabbage and mix it with a touch of salt. Set aside for 5 to 10 minutes. After this time squeeze out the liquid from your cabbage and transfer to another mixing bowl.

2. Mix your cabbage with the rest of your ingredients for your filling until thoroughly combined.

3. Next roll out your dumpling wrappers and drizzle the edges with some water.

4. Place your filling by the spoonful into the center of your wrappers and cover. Seal the edges with a fork. Repeat with remaining wrappers and filling.

5. Then place your dumplings onto a baking sheet and place into your fridge to chill for the next 30 minutes.

6. Next heat up some oil in a large skillet placed over high heat. Once the oil is simmering add in your dumplings and cook for the next couple of minutes or until brown and golden in color.

7. Then reduce the heat to low and continue cooking the dumplings for the next 6 to 8 minutes before removing from heat and enjoying whenever you are ready.

Simple Dumplings

If you want yet another traditional dumpling recipe to enjoy, then this is the perfect dish for you.

Serves: 6 Servings

Time: 20 mins.

Ingredients:

- 1 Cup of Flour, All Purpose Variety
- 2 tsp of Baker's Style Baking Powder
- 1 teaspoon of Sugar, White
- ½ tsp of Salt, For Taste
- 1 tbsp of Margarine, Soft
- ½ Cup of Milk, Whole

Directions:

1. First stir together your first 4 ingredients in a medium sized bowl. Then cut in your butter until your mixture is crumbly.

2. Stir in your milk to make a very soft dough.

3. Drop your mixture by the spoonful into a boiling stew or soup.

4. Cover and allow to cook for the next 15 minutes before serving. Enjoy.

Old Fashioned Dumplings

This dish is one of the most comforting and satisfying dishes that you will ever have the pleasure of making.

Serves: 10 to 12

Time: 1 hr.

Ingredients:

Your Soup:

- 1, 4 to 5 Pound Chicken, Whole

- 1 Onion, Yellow in Color, Medium in Size and Finely Diced
- 5 Bay Leaves, Fresh and Dried
- 5 tbsp of Butter, Unsalted Variety
- 1 ½ tbsp of Salt, For Taste
- ½ tsp of Black Pepper, For Taste

Your Dumplings:

- 3 Cups of Flour, All Purpose Variety
- 1 ½ tsp of Baker's Style Baking Powder
- 1 teaspoon of Salt, For Taste
- ½ Cup of Oil, Vegetable Variety
- ¾ Cup + 2 tbsp of Water, Warm
- 2 Eggs, Large in Size and Lightly Beaten
- Dash of Parsley, Minced and Fresh

Directions:

1. The first thing that you will want to do is make your soup. To do this place your chicken into a large sized soup pot and cover with at least half an inch of water. Then add in your onions and next 4 ingredients for your soup.

2. Cover and allow to cook over high heat until it reaches a boil. Once boiling reduce the heat to low and allow to simmer for the next hour or until your chicken is completely cooked through.

3. Once cooked remove the bay leaves from your pot and transfer your chicken to a cutting board. Shred your chicken finely with 2 forks and then return back to your soup.

4. Next make your dumplings. To do this add in your first 3 ingredients for dumplings into a large sized bowl and whisk thoroughly to blend.

5. Then add in your oil, water and eggs and stir to combine. Knead your dough with your hands until evenly mixed.

6. Next cut your dough into small sized balls and roll out your pieces into thin rectangles.

7. Drop your dumplings into your soup and allow to boil for the next 20 minutes or until your dumplings begin to rise to the surface.

8. After this time remove from heat and garnish with some parsley. Serve while still piping hot.

Chicken Dumpling Soup

These dumplings are tasty and crunchy with every bite.

Serves: 5

Time: 1½ hrs.

Ingredients:

- Wonton/ Siu Kow wrappers (20)
- Water (4 cups)

Scallion Filling:

- Mushroom- wood ear (1)
- Ground Chicken (6 oz.)
- Shrimp (4 oz., peeled and deveined)
- Water Chestnuts (2, peeled and minced)
- Green Onion (1 tbsp, chopped)

Seasoning

- Sesame Oil (1/2 teaspoon)
- Oil (1 ½ tsp)
- Shaoxing wine (1 teaspoon)
- Salt (1/2 teaspoon)
- Fish Sauce (1/2 teaspoon)
- White Pepper (1/4 tsp)
- Chicken bouillon powder (3/4 teaspoon)

Soup:

- Chicken broth (1 ¾ cups)
- Water (1 cup)
- Salt (1/4 tsp)
- Green onion (for garnish)
- White Pepper (1/4 tsp)

Directions:

1. Immerse mushrooms in lukewarm water for 15 minutes.

2. Combine all the seasoning and ingredients for filling with mushroom. Mix and chill for half hour.

3. Take a wrapper, lay it flat and fill with 1 tbsp refrigerated filling. Wet the rim of the wrapper, fold and press to seal.

4. Make sure it is sealed tightly. Repeat till wrappers are finished.

5. Set dumplings aside and use a wet cloth to cover them, keeping them moist.

6. Boil a pot of water and cook dumplings till they float, stir to avoid sticking.

7. Take dumplings from the pot, cover to keep moist. Use another pot to heat chicken broth and water. Add pepper and salt.

8. Put dumplings in a bowl, add soup and sprinkle with scallion. Serve hot.

Traditional Semmelknoedel

This dumpling recipe is a Bavarian classic that is meant to accompany flavorful dishes such as roasted pork and game dishes dripping in gravy. For the tastiest results, I highly recommend that you serve this dumpling dish with some mushrooms and gravy.

Serves: 4

Time: 50 mins.

Ingredients:

- 1 Pound of French Bread, Stale and Cut into Small Cubes
- 1 Cup of Milk, Whole
- 2 tbsp of Butter, Soft
- 1 Onion, Finely Chopped
- 1 tbsp of Parsley, Fresh and Roughly Chopped
- 2 Eggs, Large in Size and Beaten Lightly
- Dash of Black Pepper, For Taste
- ½ Cup of Bread Crumbs, Dried

Directions:

1. First place your bread cubes into a large sized bowl.

2. Then heat up your milk until it begins to boil and pour it over your bread cubes. Stir gently to coat all of your bread cubes and allow to sit for the next 15 minutes.

3. Next melt your butter in a large sized skillet placed over medium heat. Once your butter seems to be melted add in your onions and cook until they are tender to the touch.

4. Then add in your parsley and stir to combine. Remove from heat.

5. Add in your eggs with a dash of salt and pepper into your milk and bread mixture and use your hands to stir thoroughly to combine.

6. Next bring a large sized pot of water to boil and once the water begins to boil drop in your dumplings by the tbsp until all of your dough has been used up.

7. Continue to cook for the next 20 minutes before removing with a spoon and serving whenever you are ready.

Farmhouse Style Chicken and Drop Dumplings

Here is yet another soup style recipe that I know you are going to want to make.

Serves: 10 to 12

Time: 1 hr. 45 mins.

Ingredients:

Your Chicken Soup:

- 2, 3 Pound Chickens, Cut into Small Sized Pieces
- ½ Cup of Butter, Unsalted Variety and Soft

- 6 Carrots, Medium in Size and Chopped into Small Pieces
- 6 Cloves of Garlic, Sliced Thinly
- Celery, 4 Stalks, Chopped into Small Pieces
- 2 Leeks, Large in Size, White Part Only, chopped into Small Pieces and Soaked
- 2 Onions, Yellow in Color, Medium in Size and Chopped Finely
- 1 tbsp of Seasoning, Poultry Variety
- ½ Cup of Flour, All Purpose Variety

Your Dumplings:

- 2 ½ Cups of Flour, All Purpose Variety
- ¾ Cup of Milk, Whole and as Needed
- 2 tbsp of Butter, Soft
- 1 tbsp of Baker's Style Baking Powder
- 2 tsp of Salt, For Taste
- 2 Eggs, Large in Size and Beaten Lightly
- ¼ Cup of Parsley, Fresh and Roughly Chopped

Directions:

1. Place your chicken into a large sized pot filled with at least 16 cups of water and bring it to a boil.

2. Switch the heat to low then allow your chicken to cook for the next 25 to 30 minutes or until completely cooked through.

3. After this time remove your chicken and set aside for later use.

4. Once your chicken is cool to the touch shred your chicken finely with two forks and set aside.

5. Use another medium sized pot and melt your butter over medium heat. Once your butter is fully melted add in your next 6 ingredients and stir to combine.

6. Cook for the next 8 to 10 minutes or until your vegetables are tender to the touch.

7. Then add in your flour and stir to combine.

8. Next make your dumplings. To do this use a medium sized bowl and add in all of your ingredients for your dumplings. Mix until thoroughly combined.

9. Then cut your dough into smaller sized balls and drop into your soup to cook for the next 10 to 12 minutes or until they begin to float to the surface.

10. Serve and enjoy.

Turkey Style Dumplings

These dumplings are packed full of delicious flavor that I know you won't be able to get enough of.

Serves: 10

Time: 1 hr. and 10 mins.

Ingredients:

- 1 Pound of Turkey, Fully Cooked and Finely Chopped
- 3 Cups of Water, Warm

- Dash of Salt, For Taste
- Dash of Pepper, For Taste
- 3 tbsp of Flour, All Purpose Variety
- 1, 12 Ounce Pack of Biscuit Dough, Refrigerated

Directions:

1. First place your first 4 ingredients into a medium sized saucepan and bring your mixture to a boil. Once your mixture is boiling reduce your heat to low and simmer for the next 30 to 40 minutes.

2. Next spread your flour on a medium sized cutting board and roll out your dough. Cut into small sized pieces and drop these into your broth.

3. Cook over low heat for the next 40 minutes before removing from heat and serving.

Conclusion

You did it! Thank you for reading through the Simple Gyoza Recipe Cookbook. I sincerely hope that you were able to follow along with all 30 simple yet delicious dumplings and gyoza recipes. Please feel free to leave me an honest review, so I can know what your thoughts were.

Tootles!